BUNNY BRUNEL'S
XTREME!
BASS

IDEAS & EXERCISES TO
UNLOCK YOUR CREATIVITY

 Backbeat
Books

San Francisco

Published by Backbeat Books
600 Harrison Street, San Francisco, CA 94107
www.backbeatbooks.com
email: books@musicplayer.com

An imprint of CMP Information
Publishers of *Guitar Player*, *Bass Player*, *Keyboard*, and *EQ* magazines

CMP
United Business Media

Distributed to the book trade in the US and Canada by
Publishers Group West, 1700 Fourth Street, Berkeley, CA 94710

Distributed to the music trade in the US and Canada by
Hal Leonard Publishing, P.O. Box 13819, Milwaukee, WI 53213

Text design and composition by Chris Ledgerwood
Music engraving by Elizabeth Ledgerwood
Cover design and front cover photo by Paul Haggard

ISBN 0-87930-795-1

Printed in the United States of America

05 06 07 08 09   5 4 3 2 1

This book is dedicated to Emmy and Gigi.

Contents

Introduction   7

Notational Symbols   9

Lesson 1   Xtreme! Exercises   11

Lesson 2   *C* Major Modes: Extended Patterns/Positions   23

Lesson 3   Xtreme! Exercise Examples with the Extended Patterns/Positions   31

Lesson 4   *C* Harmonic Minor Modes: Extended Patterns/Positions   35

Lesson 5   *C* Melodic Minor Modes: Extended Patterns/Positions   45

Lesson 6   *C* Harmonic Major Modes: Extended Patterns/Positions   55

Lesson 7   Additional Modes: Extended Patterns/Positions   63

Lesson 8   Chord Embellishments and Arpeggio Extensions   67

Lesson 9   Playing Arpeggios on the Bass: *C* Major Patterns/Positions   73

Lesson 10   *C* Harmonic Minor Modes: Arpeggio Patterns/Positions   83

Lesson 11   *C* Melodic Minor Modes: Arpeggio Patterns/Positions   93

Lesson 12   *C* Harmonic Major Modes: Arpeggio Patterns/Positions   101

Lesson 13   Additional Modes: Arpeggio Patterns/Positions   111

Lesson 14   Xtreme! Exercise Examples for Arpeggios   115

Lesson 15   Where to Use the Modes   119

On the CD   121

Acknowledgments   123

About the Author   125

Introduction

Are you tired of playing the same boring exercises over and over? Do you feel that you are not progressing anymore? Have you lost the direction you had when you set out to become a great bass player? Do you wish you had some idea of what to do next?

Well, your wish has come true!

Xtreme! Bass will set you on a new course. My Xtreme! exercises will help you get over the hump. You will learn new scales, new fingerings, new patterns, and new ideas.

When I started playing the bass in the '60s, I used to pick up lines by ear from records by artists like James Brown, Otis Redding, and Blood Sweat & Tears, as well as by Ray Brown and Ron Carter. Later on, after listening to solos from Eddie Gomez and Stanley Clarke, I decided to start practicing my bass eight to ten hours a day. My goal was to be able to play solos on the bass like John Coltrane or Herbie Hancock do on their instruments. Because there was no precedent for that style of bass playing, I had to invent new fingerings and techniques to achieve my goal.

In the end, I developed new ways to play intervals and phrases that sound closer to the sax or the piano. In this book I help you master these ideas for playing phrases that seem impossible on the bass.

In *Xtreme! Bass* I'll first show you basic patterns and then some extended fingerings that you can apply to those patterns. These will get your fingers "thinking" in new ways on the fretboard. We'll then explore different modes and arpeggios in various patterns and positions—once you learn the patterns/positions, be sure to play through the modes in every key and then apply the modes to the basic patterns you learned in Lesson 1. Finally, I'll show you how the different modes fit with the chord forms you'll find in jazz and pop music.

As you work through the lessons in *Xtreme! Bass*, you'll find your "finger intelligence" expanding so you won't be bound by those familiar scale and interval relationships that make your soloing seem stale. To take full advantage of this knowledge, be sure to *listen* to the fresh new sounds the exercises produce, so that they become part of your musical as well as your fretboard vocabulary. Listening to the tracks on the CD will help you internalize these sounds.

As with any kind of practice, be sure to warm up and start slowly when you play the lessons in *Xtreme! Bass*. As you grow more confident, gradually increase the speed on your metronome or drum program, always making sure to give your hands a rest *before* any aches or twinges appear.

Ultimately, the new sounds and approaches you'll learn in *Xtreme! Bass* will become second nature, so that when you play you can concentrate on what's most important—making great music.

Notational Symbols

Backbeat Books uses the following symbols to indicate fingerings and techniques.

Slide (capital S): If the notes are tied, pluck only the first. When there is no tie, pluck both notes.

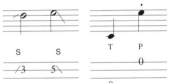

A slide symbol before or after a single note indicates a slide to or from an unspecific pitch.

A **thumb slap** is indicated with a capital T; a **pop** by a capital P.

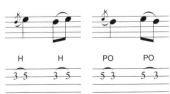 

Capital H indicates a **hammer-on**.

Capital PO indicates a **pull-off**.

Harmonics are indicated by tiny circles over the note heads, which indicate actual pitch; the tablature shows where the harmonic is played.

Capital B indicates a **bend**, either from a grace-note or a note with a full duration value.

Capital R indicates a **release**: Pre-bend to the note in parentheses, play, and then release the bend to the indicated note.

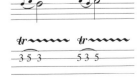 

Finger vibrato.

Trill.

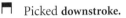

Picked **downstroke.**

V Picked **upstroke.**

4 **Fretting-hand fingerings** are indicated by numerals. (1=index finger, 2=middle finger, etc.).

How Tablature Works.
The horizontal lines represent the bass strings, the bottom line being *E* and the top being *G*. Numbers designate the frets (0 indicates an open string). For instance, a 2 positioned on the bottom line would mean play the 2nd fret on the *E* string. Time values are shown in the standard notation directly above the tablature. Special symbols and instructions appear between the notation and tablature staves.

Xtreme! Exercises

The following are exercises you should get familiar with. I recommend practicing them until you understand the idea behind the patterns. Practice them with familiar scales before getting into the Xtreme! fingering of Lesson 2.

The Patterns

- **Example 1-1:** *C* major scale
- **Example 1-2:** *C* major scale doubling the notes
- **Example 1-3:** 3rds
- **Example 1-4:** 3rds doubling the notes
- **Example 1-5:** Four-note pattern
- **Example 1-6:** Four-note pattern doubling the notes
- **Example 1-7:** Xtreme! endurance exercise 1
- **Example 1-8:** Xtreme! endurance exercise 2
- **Example 1-9:** Xtreme! endurance exercise 3
- **Example 1-10:** 3rds backward
- **Example 1-11:** 3rds, one up, one down
- **Example 1-12:** Four-note pattern backward
- **Example 1-13:** Four-note pattern, one up, one down
- **Example 1-14:** Four-note pattern and arpeggio down
- **Example 1-15:** Arpeggios up and down
- **Example 1-16:** Double-note funk pattern
- **Example 1-17:** Quadruple-note funk pattern

I will start by showing you the basic exercises using a simple and easy *C* major fingering pattern in the middle of the neck. That will let you warm up before getting Xtreme! We will be using the same exercises with all the modes and scales. Figure 1-1 charts the scale on a 4-string bass, Fig. 1-2 on a 5-string.

C Major Scale

Ex. 1-1

TRACK ①

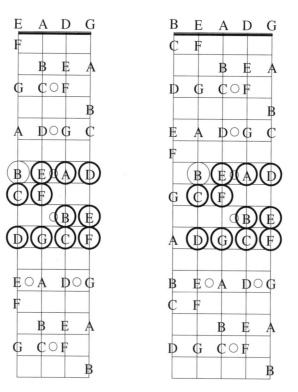

Fig. 1-1 and Fig. 1-2

C Major Scale Doubling the Notes

Ex. 1-2

TRACK  2

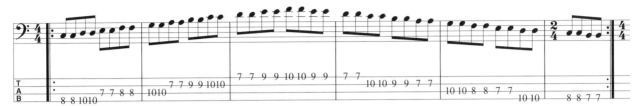

3rds

Ex. 1-3

TRACK 3

3rds Doubling the Notes

Ex. 1-4

TRACK 4

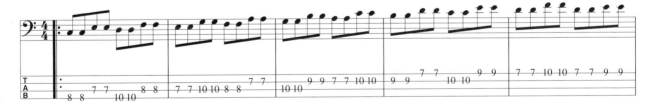

Four-note Pattern

TRACK 5

Ex. 1-5

Four-note Pattern Doubling the Notes

TRACK 6

Ex. 1-6

Xtreme! Endurance

The following three exercises are very good for developing Xtreme! endurance.

Xtreme! Endurance Exercise 1
Ex. 1-7

Xtreme! Endurance Exercise 2
Ex. 1-8

TRACK 8

Xtreme! Endurance Exercise 3
Ex. 1-9

TRACK 9

3rds Backward

TRACK 10

Ex. 1-10

3rds, One Up, One Down

TRACK 11

Ex. 1-11

Four-note Pattern Backward

TRACK 12

Ex. 1-12

Four-note Pattern, One Up, One Down

Ex. 1-13

Four-note Pattern and Arpeggio Down

Ex. 1-14

TRACK **14**

Arpeggios Up and Down

Ex. 1-15

Double-note Funk Pattern

I recorded this example at four different tempos. You should practice all of the exercises the same way.

Ex. 1-16

Quadruple-note Funk Pattern

Ex. 1-17

C Major Modes:
Extended Patterns/Positions

These next patterns and positions will stretch your fingers a lot. For that reason I recommend practicing them gradually every day. You have been used to playing with one finger per fret—now you will be playing some portions of the scales with two frets per finger! I call the next patterns "extended" because they cover two modes at the same time.

The Patterns/Positions

- **Examples 2-1, 2-2:** *B* Locrian and *C* Ionian extended

  The Locrian pattern goes over m7♭5 (half-diminished) chords. In this case it would go with *Bm7♭5*.

- **Examples 2-3, 2-4:** *C* Ionian and *D* Dorian extended

  The Ionian pattern goes over major chords, in this case with *C, Cmaj7, Cmaj9,* or *C6,* but only if *C* is the tonic of the key.

- **Examples 2-5, 2-6:** *D* Dorian and *E* Phrygian extended

  The Dorian pattern goes with minor chords, in this case with *Dm, Dm7, Dm6, Dm11,* and *Dm13.*

- **Examples 2-7, 2-8:** *E* Phrygian and *F* Lydian extended

  The Phrygian pattern goes over minor chords—in this case *Em* and *Em7*—but only when the root of the chord is the 3rd of the key. Example: *Am7* in the key of *F.*

- **Examples 2-9, 2-10:** *F* Lydian and *G* Mixolydian extended

  The Lydian pattern goes with major chords, in this case with *F* major, *Fmaj7, F6,* and *Fmaj9.*

- **Examples 2-11, 2-12:** *G* Mixolydian and *A* Aeolian extended

  The Mixolydian pattern goes with dominant chords, in this case with *G7, G11, G13,* and *G9.*

- **Examples 2-13, 2-14:** *A* Aeolian and *B* Locrian extended

  The Aeolian pattern goes with minor chords when the tonic of the chord is the relative minor, or 6th, of the key. In this case, in the key of *C* major, it would go with *Am, Am7,* and *Am9.*

B Locrian and *C* Ionian
Extended Pattern/Position

TRACK 21

Ex. 2-1

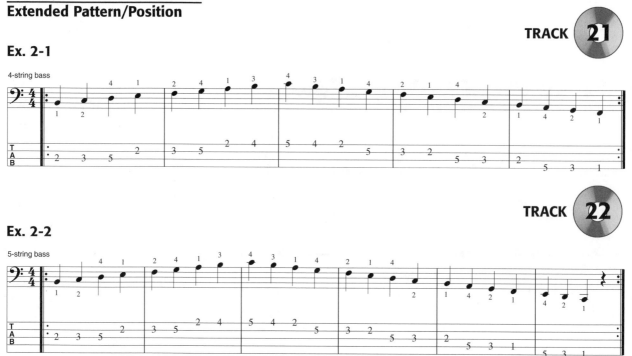

TRACK 22

Ex. 2-2

Fig. 2-1 and Fig. 2-2

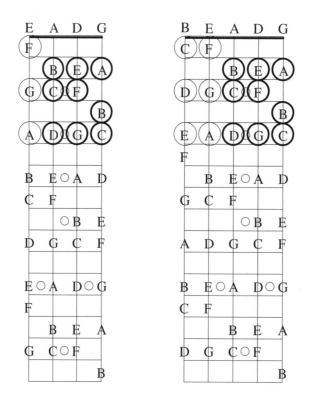

C Ionian and *D* Dorian
Extended Pattern/Position

TRACK 23

Ex. 2-3

TRACK 24

Ex. 2-4

Fig. 2-3 and Fig. 2-4

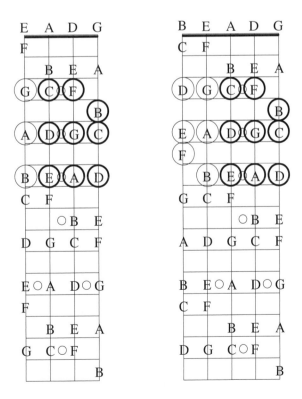

_D_ Dorian and _E_ Phrygian
Extended Pattern/Position

TRACK 25

Ex. 2-5

TRACK 26

Ex. 2-6

Fig. 2-5 and Fig. 2-6

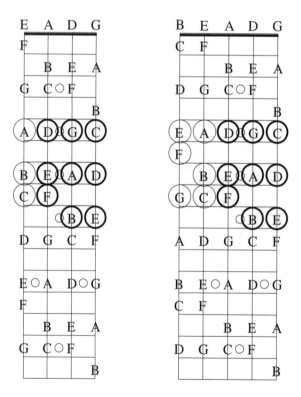

E Phrygian and *F* Lydian
Extended Pattern/Position

TRACK 27

Ex. 2-7

TRACK 28

Ex. 2-8

Fig. 2-7 and Fig. 2-8

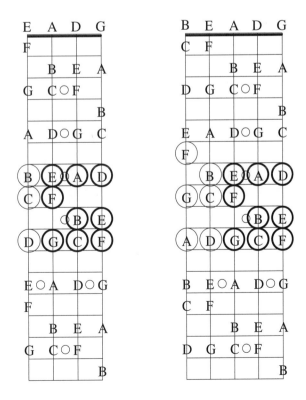

F Lydian and *G* Mixolydian
Extended Pattern/Position

TRACK 29

Ex. 2-9

TRACK 30

Ex. 2-10

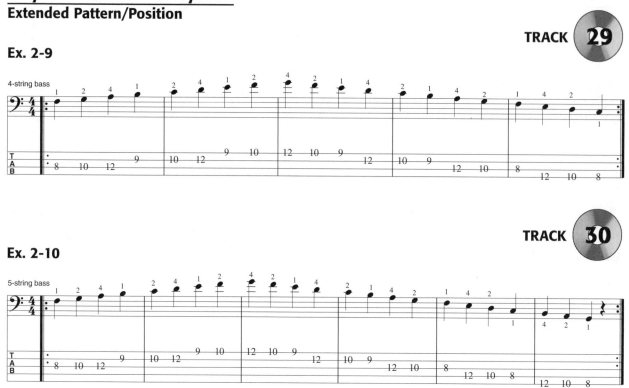

Fig. 2-9 and Fig. 2-10

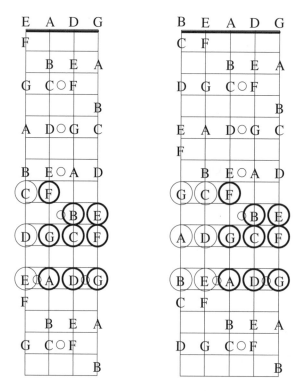

G Mixolydian and *A* Aeolian
Extended Pattern/Position

TRACK 31

Ex. 2-11

TRACK 32

Ex. 2-12

Fig. 2-11 and Fig. 2-12

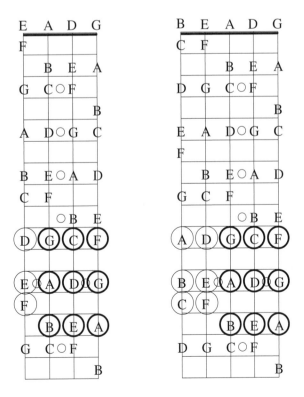

A Aeolian and *B* Locrian
Extended Pattern/Position

TRACK 33

Ex. 2-13

Ex. 2-14

TRACK 34

Fig. 2-13 and Fig. 2-14

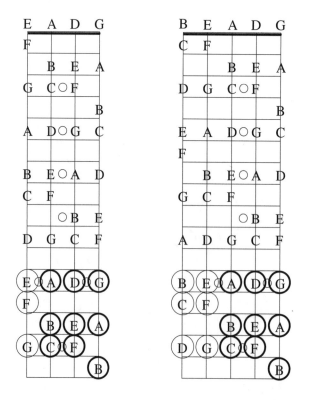

Xtreme! Exercise Examples
with the Extended Patterns/Positions

Before we go on to the next set of modes I would like to demonstrate some of the Xtreme! exercises from the first lesson as applied to the extended patterns/positions. You will notice after doing just one run that it really stretches your fingers. This will help your technique considerably, but to avoid injuring yourself do not practice too long at the beginning. Like any repetitive practice, if you practice too long you may develop tendinitis.

The Patterns

- **Example 3-1:** 3rds
- **Example 3-2:** Four-note pattern
- **Example 3-3:** Four-note pattern doubling the notes
- **Example 3-4:** 3rds doubling the notes
- **Example 3-5:** 3rds backward
- **Example 3-6:** 3rds, one up, one down
- **Example 3-7:** Four-note pattern backward
- **Example 3-8:** Four-note pattern, one up, one down

There are an infinite number of exercises we can come up with, but I think that it is better to master a small number of exercises before trying new ones. In this case I chose eight exercises based on patterns that are used the most often in Western music. That will give you great technique control, which will enable you to explore different exercises later.

3rds

TRACK 35

Ex. 3-1

Four-note Pattern

TRACK 36

Ex. 3-2

Four-note Pattern Doubling the Notes

TRACK 37

Ex. 3-3

3rds Doubling the Notes

TRACK 38

Ex. 3-4

3rds Backward

TRACK 39

Ex. 3-5

3rds, One Up, One Down

TRACK 40

Ex. 3-6

Four-note Pattern Backward

TRACK 41

Ex. 3-7

Four-note Pattern, One Up, One Down

TRACK 42

Ex. 3-8

C Harmonic Minor Modes:
Extended Patterns/Positions

Scholars have often asked me why in my system the first mode of the harmonic minor modes—the Ionian harmonic minor—was not the harmonic minor scale that they learned in school. That traditional harmonic minor mode has a minor 3rd and minor 6th but a major 7th, so that C harmonic minor is spelled *C–D–E♭–F–G–A♭–B–C*.

The answer is that in my system the harmonic minor modes are based on the 6th of the key—the Aeolian harmonic minor—instead of the Ionian. This leaves the order of the modes in the same key as the major modes. In short, the harmonic minor scale is simply an Aeolian scale with a major 7th! That means the key of C, the Aeolian harmonic minor is *A–B–C–D–E–F–G♯–A*. Starting the mode on C (Ionian harmonic minor), we get *C–D–E–F–G♯–A–B–C*; starting on D (Dorian harmonic minor), *D–E–F–G♯–A–B–C–D*, and so on through the modes.

The Patterns/Positions

- **Examples 4-1, 4-2:** *B* Locrian and *C* Ionian harmonic minor extended
- **Examples 4-3, 4-4:** *C* Ionian and *D* Dorian harmonic minor extended
- **Examples 4-5, 4-6:** *D* Dorian and *E* Phrygian harmonic minor extended
- **Examples 4-7, 4-8:** *E* Phrygian and *F* Lydian harmonic minor extended

    I like to call the Phrygian harmonic minor the "Spanish Phrygian"—it has a definite Spanish sound. This harmonic minor mode is the one used the most frequently in improvisation. The Spanish Phrygian is used for dominant-7th chords when the tonic of that chord is the 3rd of the key. In this case, in the key of C major it would go with: *E7, E7♭9, E7♭13*, and *E7♯5*.

- **Examples 4-9, 4-10:** *E* Phrygian to *F* Lydian harmonic minor alternative
- **Examples 4-11, 4-12:** *F* Lydian and *G♯* Mixolydian harmonic minor extended
- **Examples 4-13, 4-14:** *G♯* Mixolydian and *A* Aeolian harmonic minor extended

    The Mixolydian harmonic minor is a good substitute mode with diminished chords. In this case it would go with *G♯dim* or *G♯dim7*.

- **Examples 4-15, 4-16:** *A* Aeolian and *B* Locrian harmonic minor extended
- **Examples 4-17, 4-18:** *A* Aeolian to *B* Locrian harmonic minor alternative

    The Aeolian harmonic minor is used for minor/major 7th chords when the tonic of the chord is the relative minor, or 6th, of the key. In this case, in the key of C major it would go with *Am/maj7* or *Am/maj9*.

B Locrian and *C* Ionian Harmonic Minor
Extended Pattern/Position

TRACK **43**

Ex. 4-1

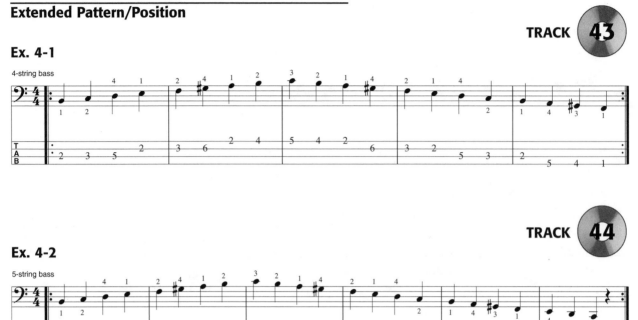

TRACK **44**

Ex. 4-2

Fig. 4-1 and Fig. 4-2

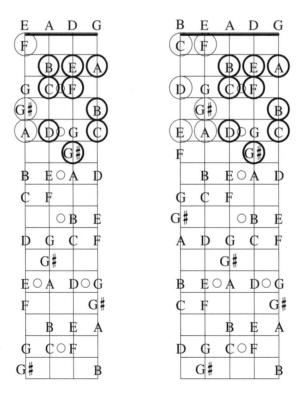

C Ionian and *D* Dorian Harmonic Minor

Extended Pattern/Position

TRACK 45

Ex. 4-3

TRACK 46

Ex. 4-4

Fig. 4-3 and Fig. 4-4

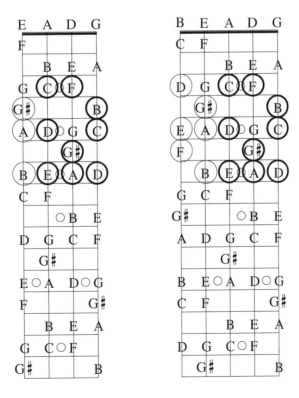

D Dorian and *E* Phrygian Harmonic Minor
Extended Pattern/Position

TRACK 47

Ex. 4-5

TRACK 48

Ex. 4-6

Fig. 4-5 and Fig. 4-6

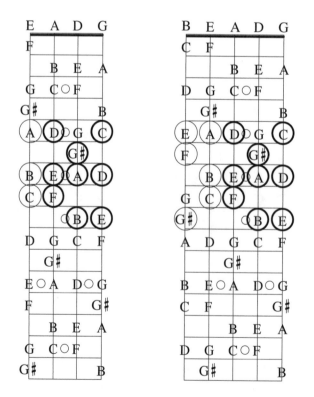

E Phrygian and *F* Lydian Harmonic Minor
Extended Pattern/Position

TRACK 49

Ex. 4-7

Ex. 4-8

TRACK 50

Fig. 4-7 and Fig. 4-8

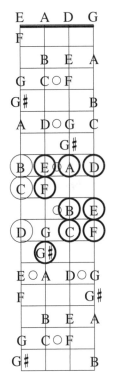 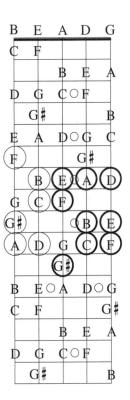

E Phrygian to *F* Lydian Harmonic Minor
Alternative Extended Pattern/Position

TRACK **51**

Ex. 4-9

Ex. 4-10

TRACK **52**

Fig. 4-9 and Fig. 4-10

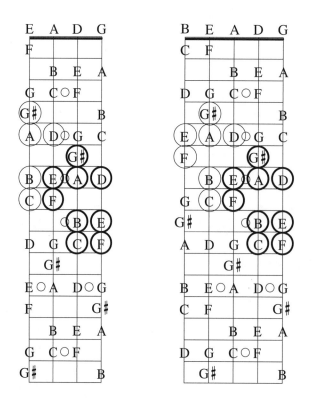

F Lydian and *G♯* Mixolydian Harmonic Minor
Extended Pattern/Position

TRACK 53

Ex. 4-11

TRACK 54

Ex. 4-12

Fig. 4-11 and Fig. 4-12

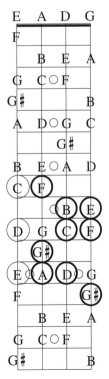
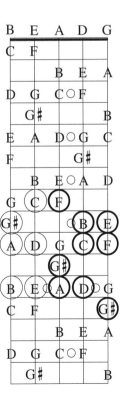

G# Mixolydian and *A* Aeolian Harmonic Minor
Extended Pattern/Position

TRACK 55

Ex. 4-13

Ex. 4-14

TRACK 56

Fig. 4-13 and Fig. 4-14

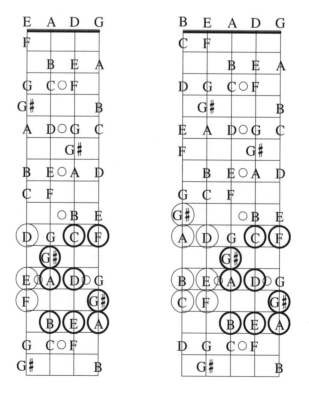

A Aeolian and *B* Locrian Harmonic Minor

Extended Pattern/Position

TRACK 57

Ex. 4-15

TRACK 58

Ex. 4-16

Fig. 4-15 and Fig. 4-16

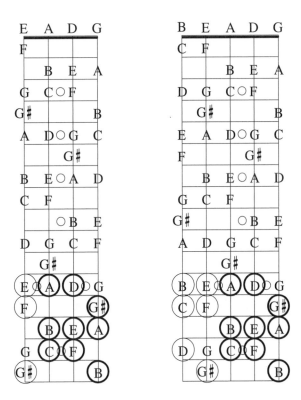

A Aeolian to *B* Locrian Harmonic Minor
Alternative Extended Pattern/Position

TRACK **59**

Ex. 4-17

TRACK **60**

Ex. 4-18

Fig. 4-17 and Fig. 4-18

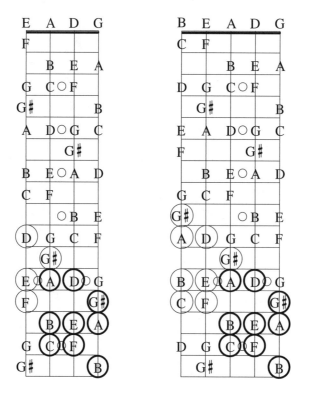

C Melodic Minor Modes:
Extended Patterns/Positions

The mystery of the melodic minor scale that we learn in music school: In the beginning, scholars tried to make it fit in Baroque music as the 6th mode of a key, along with the natural minor (Aeolian), spelled one way going up the scale and another (like the natural minor) coming down—for instance, C–D–E♭–F–G–A–B–C; C–B♭–A♭–G–F–E♭–D–C. Later on Béla Bartók declared that the scale was not the 6th of the key but was in fact the No. 1 mode of its own key, and he started composing new melodies using only the melodic minor scale. The most famous of these compositions are called *Mikrokosmos* (*Microcosms*). For that reason we still learn the melodic minor modes starting with the Ionian melodic minor as the No. 1 mode, when this mode in regard to the key is actually a Dorian (No. 2) mode with a major 7.

The Patterns/Positions

- **Examples 5-1, 5-2:** *B* Super Locrian and *C* Ionian melodic minor extended
- **Examples 5-3, 5-4:** *B* Super Locrian to *E♭* Phrygian melodic minor alternative
  I also call the Super Locrian the *altered scale*. This mode goes with altered chords, in this case with *Balt*, *B7♯5♯9*, *B7♭5♭9*, etc.
- **Examples 5-5, 5-6:** *C* Ionian and *D* Dorian melodic minor extended
  The Ionian melodic minor goes with minor/major 7th chords, in this case with *Cm/maj7* or *Cm/maj9*.
- **Examples 5-7, 5-8:** *D* Dorian and *E♭* Phrygian melodic minor extended
  The Dorian melodic minor goes with minor 7♭9 chords, in this case with *Dm7♭9*.
- **Examples 5-9, 5-10:** *E♭* Phrygian and *F* Lydian melodic minor extended
  The Phrygian melodic minor goes with major 7♯5 chords, in this case with *E♭maj7♯5* or *E♭maj9♯5*.
- **Examples 5-11, 5-12:** *F* Lydian/Mixolydian and *G* Mixolydian melodic minor extended
  The Lydian/Mixolydian goes with dominant 7♯11 or ♭5 chords, in this case with *F7♭5* or *F7♯11*.
- **Examples 5-13, 5-14:** *F* Lydian/Mixolydian to *A* Aeolian melodic minor alternative
- **Examples 5-15, 5-16:** *G* Super Mixolydian and *A* Aeolian melodic minor extended
  I like to call the Super Mixolydian the ♭13 scale. It goes with ♭13 chords, in this case with *G7♭13*.
- **Examples 5-17, 5-18:** *A* Aeolian and *B* Locrian melodic minor extended
  The Aeolian melodic minor goes with minor 7♭5 chords with a 9, in this case with *Am7♭5/9*.

B Super Locrian and *C* Ionian Melodic Minor
Extended Pattern/Position

TRACK 61

Ex. 5-1

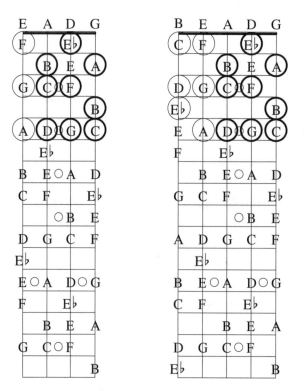

TRACK 62

Ex. 5-2

Fig. 5-1 and Fig. 5-2

B Super Locrian to *E♭* Phrygian Melodic Minor
Alternative Extended Pattern/Position

TRACK **63**

Ex. 5-3

4-string bass

TRACK **64**

Ex. 5-4

5-string bass

Fig. 5-3 and Fig. 5-4

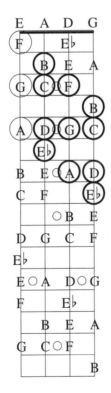
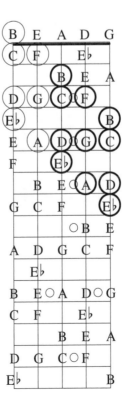

C Ionian and *D* Dorian Melodic Minor

Extended Pattern/Position

TRACK 65

Ex. 5-5

4-string bass

TRACK 66

Ex. 5-6

5-string bass

Fig. 5-5 and Fig. 5-6

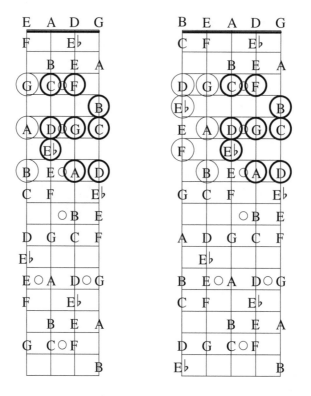

D Dorian and *E♭* Phrygian Melodic Minor
Extended Pattern/Position

TRACK 67

Ex. 5-7

TRACK 68

Ex. 5-8

Fig. 5-7 and Fig. 5-8

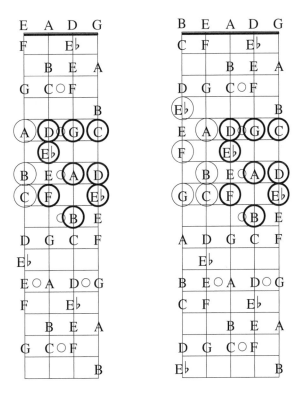

E♭ Phrygian and *F* Lydian Melodic Minor
Extended Pattern/Position

Ex. 5-9

TRACK **69**

Ex. 5-10

TRACK **70**

Fig. 5-9 and Fig. 5-10

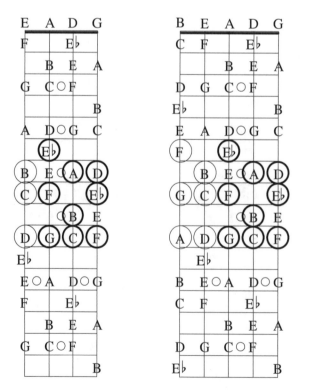

F Lydian/Mixolydian and *G* Mixolydian Melodic Minor
Extended Pattern/Position

Ex. 5-11

Ex. 5-12

Fig. 5-11 and Fig. 5-12

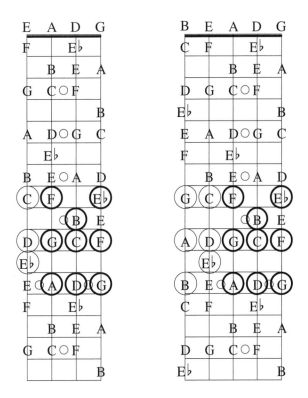

F Lydian/Mixolydian to *A* Aeolian Melodic Minor
Alternative Extended Pattern/Position

TRACK **73**

Ex. 5-13

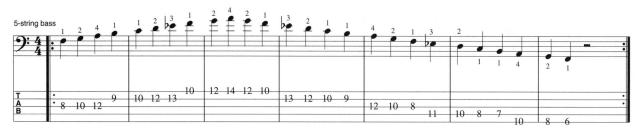

TRACK **74**

Ex. 5-14

Fig. 5-13 and Fig. 5-14

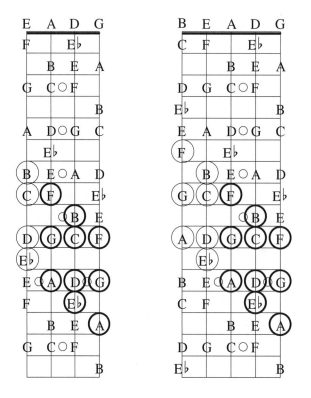

G Super Mixolydian and *A* Aeolian Melodic Minor
Extended Pattern/Position

TRACK **75**

Ex. 5-15

TRACK **76**

Ex. 5-16

Fig. 5-15 and Fig. 5-16

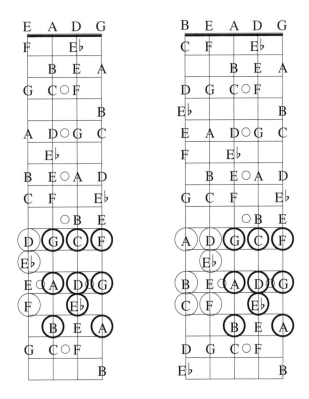

A Aeolian and *B* Locrian Melodic Minor
Extended Pattern/Position

TRACK 77

Ex. 5-17

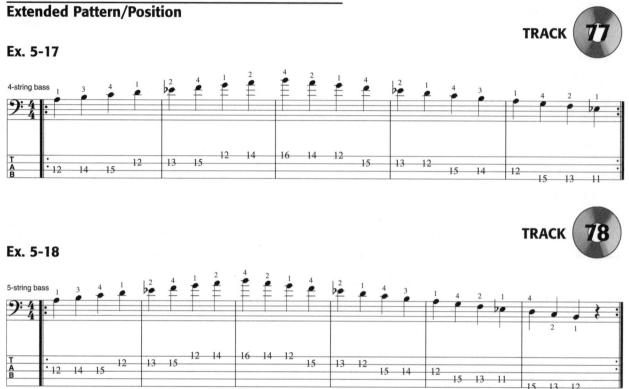

TRACK 78

Ex. 5-18

Fig. 5-17 and Fig. 5-18

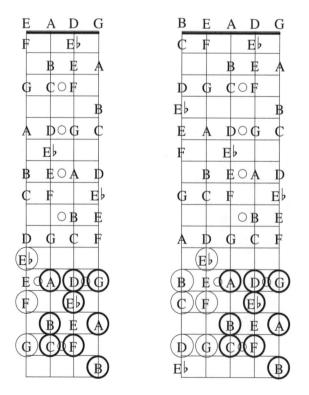

C Harmonic Major Modes:
Extended Patterns/Positions

I n my quest for learning music, a while back I discovered some scales that I could not find in any book or method. I divided them into modes that I logically positioned in the same key as the major modes. Then I called few a musician friends to ask if they knew the names for these modes. The only answer I got was from pianist Kei Akagi, who said, "I think these are called 'Egyptian' modes." I found this to be a little too vague—I am sure Egyptians have more scales than these! Playing the first one again, I noticed that it looked like the harmonic minor scale (Aeolian harmonic minor) with a major 3rd—in C Ionian mode the harmonic major is spelled C–D–E–F–G–A♭–B–C. So I decided to call these the *harmonic major modes*.

The Patterns/Positions

- **Examples 6-1, 6-2:** *B* Locrian and *C* Ionian harmonic major extended
- **Examples 6-3, 6-4:** *C* Ionian and *D* Dorian harmonic major extended
- **Examples 6-5, 6-6:** *D* Dorian and *E* Phrygian harmonic major extended
- **Examples 6-7, 6-8:** *E* Phrygian and *F* Lydian harmonic major extended

  The Phrygian harmonic major mode goes with 7th chords when the root of that chord is the 3rd of the key. In this case, in the key of *C* major, it would go with *E7, E7♭9, E7♯9, E7♭13*, or *E7♯5♯9*.

- **Examples 6-9, 6-10:** *F* Lydian and *G* Mixolydian harmonic major extended

  The Lydian harmonic major goes with major 7♯11 chords. It is a Lydian scale with a minor 3rd. In this case it would go with *Fm/maj7♯11*. Note that this chord can be mistaken for a diminished/major 7 chord.

- **Examples 6-11, 6-12:** *G* Mixolydian and *A♭* Aeolian harmonic major extended

  The Mixolydian harmonic major goes with 7♭9 chords, in this case with *G7♭9*.

- **Examples 6-13, 6-14:** *A♭* Aeolian and *B* Locrian harmonic major extended.

B Locrian and *C* Ionian Harmonic Major
Extended Pattern/Position

TRACK **79**

Ex. 6-1

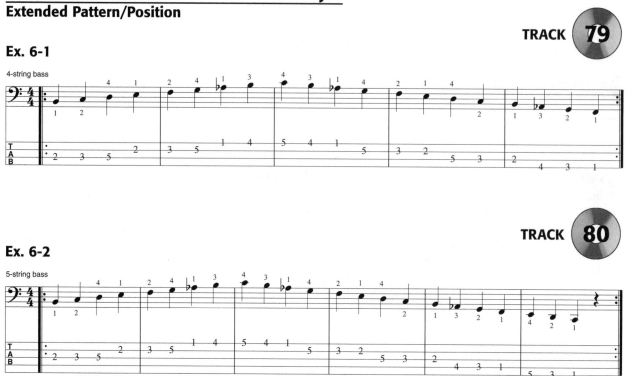

TRACK **80**

Ex. 6-2

Fig. 6-1 and Fig. 6-2

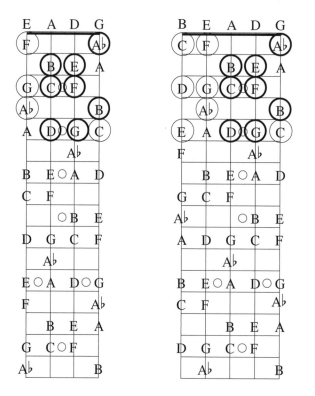

C Ionian and *D* Dorian Harmonic Major
Extended Pattern/Position

TRACK 81

Ex. 6-3

TRACK 82

Ex. 6-4

Fig. 6-3 and Fig. 6-4

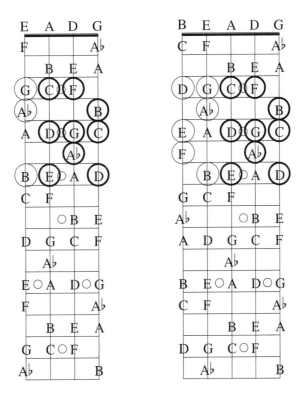

D Dorian and *E* Phrygian Harmonic Major
Extended Pattern/Position

Ex. 6-5

TRACK 83

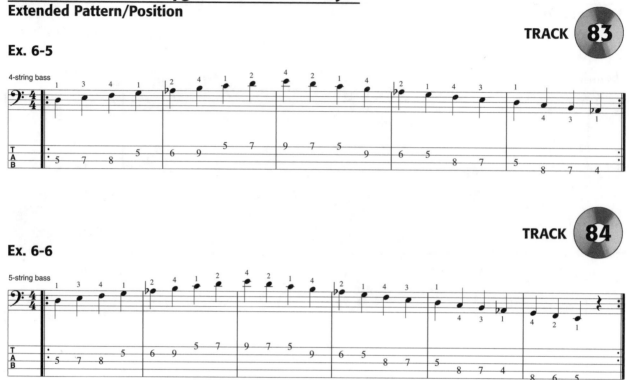

Ex. 6-6

TRACK 84

Fig. 6-5 and Fig. 6-6

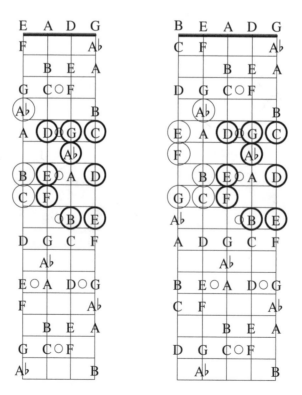

E Phrygian and *F* Lydian Harmonic Major
Extended Pattern/Position

TRACK 85

Ex. 6-7

TRACK 86

Ex. 6-8

Fig. 6-7 and Fig. 6-8

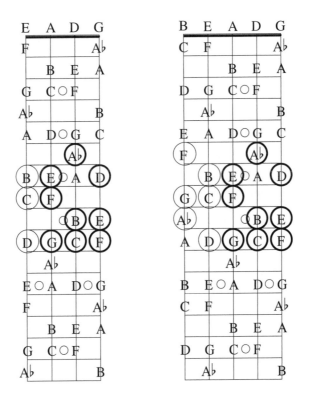

F Lydian and *G* Mixolydian Harmonic Major
Extended Pattern/Position

TRACK 87

Ex. 6-9

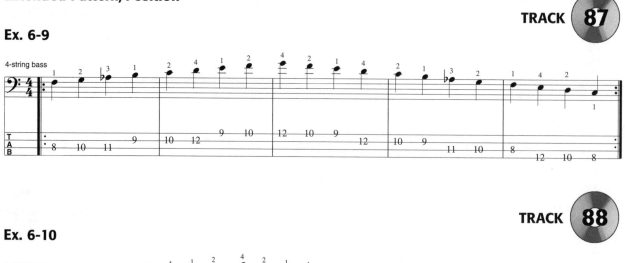

TRACK 88

Ex. 6-10

Fig. 6-9 and Fig. 6-10

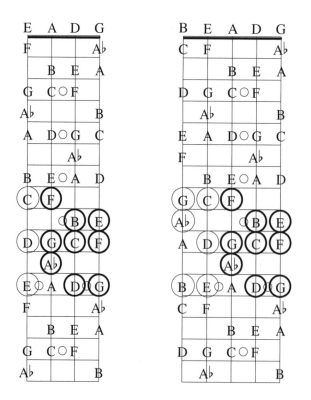

G Mixolydian and *A♭* Aeolian Harmonic Major
Extended Pattern/Position

Ex. 6-11

Ex. 6-12

Fig. 6-11 and Fig. 6-12

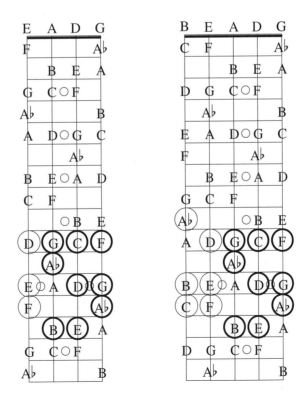

A♭ Aeolian and *B* Locrian Harmonic Major
Extended Pattern/Position

Ex. 6-13

TRACK **91**

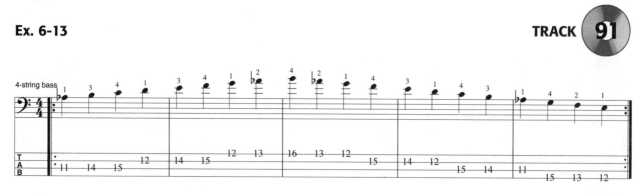

Ex. 6-14

TRACK **92**

Fig. 6-13 and Fig. 6-14

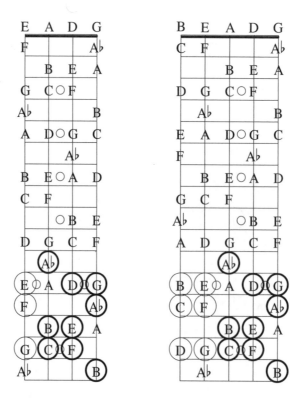

Additional Modes:
Extended Patterns/Positions

Some chords in jazz require scales that do not belong to any key. That's when these additional modes come in handy!

The Patterns/Positions

- **Examples 7-1, 7-2:** *C* diminished extended

   Guitarist Larry Coryell claims that 20th-century Russian composer Dimitri Shostakovich introduced this scale into classical music. The diminished scale goes with diminished chords. In this case it would go with *Cdim*, *Cdim7*, and *Cdim/maj7*.

- **Examples 7-3, 7-4:** *C* auxiliary diminished extended

   The auxiliary diminished scale was introduced into jazz in the bebop period. It goes with 7♭9 or 7♯9 chords, in this case with *C7♭9*, *C7♯9*, *C13♭9*, and *C13♯9*.

- **Examples 7-5, 7-6:** *C* whole-tone extended

   French Impressionist composers Claude Debussy and Maurice Ravel loved this scale. It goes with augmented chords, in this case with *Caug* and *C7♯5*. You can hear this scale very clearly at the beginning of Stevie Wonder's song "You Are the Sunshine of My Life."

C Diminished
Extended Pattern/Position

TRACK 93

Ex. 7-1

Ex. 7-2

TRACK 94

Fig. 7-1 and Fig. 7-2

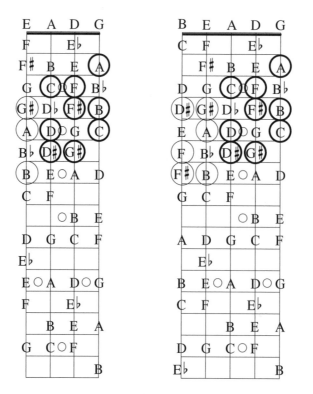

C Auxiliary Diminished
Extended Pattern/Position

TRACK 95

Ex. 7-3

Ex. 7-4

TRACK 96

Fig. 7-3 and Fig. 7-4

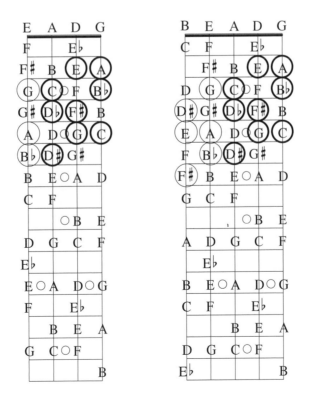

C Whole-Tone
Extended Pattern/Position

TRACK 97

Ex. 7-5

TRACK 98

Ex. 7-6

Fig. 7-5 and Fig. 7-6

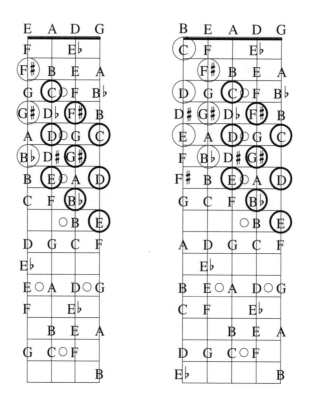

Chord Embellishments and Arpeggio Extensions

Note: For this chapter I recommend using a keyboard. Let's look first at the basic arpeggio principles. The Dictionary of Terms in Rupert Hughes's *Music Lovers' Encyclopedia* defines arpeggio as "the playing of the notes of a chord(s), one after the another, in a harp style, ripplingly."

The order of the notes in an arpeggio can be changed to create different musical effects. For simplicity, I will use only ascending and descending sequences. We'll start with the most common type of arpeggio, playing the notes of a *Cmaj7* chord (Ex. 8-1). Note that I've written the chords in bass clef, but on the CD they're played in treble clef in a more typical piano register.

TRACK 99

Ex. 8-1

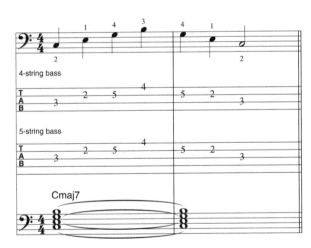

Here's the same idea over a two-octave range (Ex. 8-2).

TRACK 100

Ex. 8-2

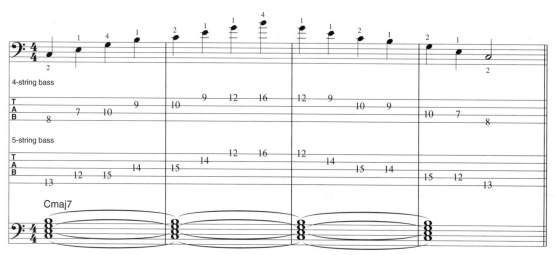

Another way of creating arpeggios is to use the chord's corresponding mode (see Lesson 15) and, from a two-octave scale, play every other note in intervals of 3rds.

To make it simple here we'll use only the major modes with their corresponding chords (Examples 8-3 through 8-9).

Arpeggio Extensions, Key of C Major

Ex. 8-3

TRACK 101

C Ionian, two octaves   **Extended arpeggio**

D Dorian

Ex. 8-4

E Phrygian

Ex. 8-5

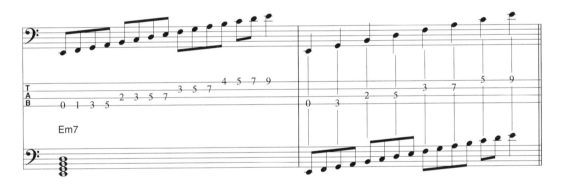

F Lydian

Ex. 8-6

G Mixolydian

Ex. 8-7

A Aeolian

Ex. 8-8

B Locrian

Ex. 8-9

Superimposed Chords

You'll notice that the chord created by these arpeggios consists of two chords superimposed. The great pianist Bill Evans used this kind of superimposition frequently. In fact, his system explains how it's possible to create chordal embellishments by adding notes of the mode to a chord. Examples 8-10 and 8-11 show the spellings of superimposed chords in the major modes. Note that the order of the notes can be changed to create different inversions.

TRACK

Ex. 8-10

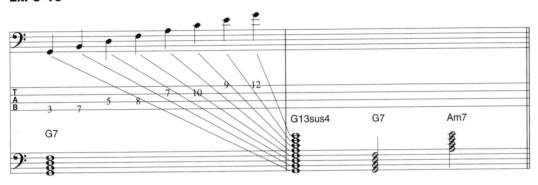

TRACK

Ex. 8-11

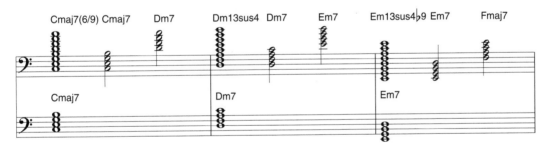

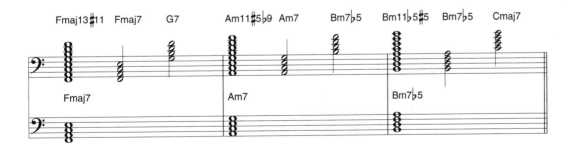

Adapting the System to the Bass

Because of the nature of the bass I found it more practical to play the upper part of an extended arpeggio one octave lower. Examples 8-12 through 8-14 show how this works in *C* Ionian.

TRACKS 110-111

Ex. 8-12   Ex. 8-13   Ex. 8-14

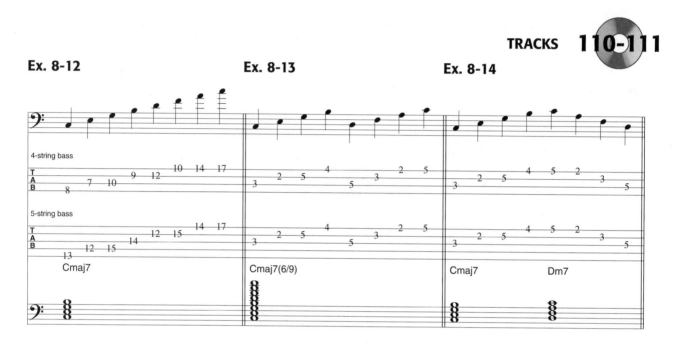

The previous examples are based on two-octave scales. Within the boundaries of your instrument and following the patterns/positions of my method, you will be able to add more extensions to each arpeggio (Examples 8-15 and 8-16).

TRACKS 113-114

Ex. 8-15   Ex. 8-16

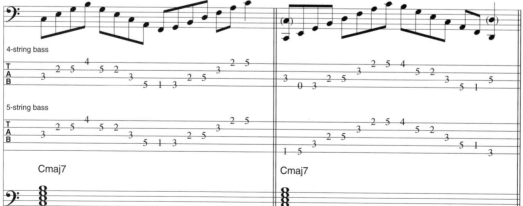

Playing Arpeggios on the Bass:
C Major Patterns/Positions

In these examples I will show the arpeggio system using *C* major. You can use the arpeggios in conjunction with chords to create bass lines and phrases and melodies for improvisation. The same way we matched the chords with the modes, we will match the arpeggios with the chords.

The Patterns/Positions

- **Examples 9-1 through 9-4:** *C* Ionian and *B* Locrian arpeggio

  The Locrian pattern goes over m7♭5 (half-diminished) chords. In this case it would go with *Bm7♭5*.

- **Examples 9-5, 9-6:** *C* Ionian alternative arpeggio

  The Ionian pattern goes over major chords, in this case with *C* major, *Cmaj7*, *Cmaj9*, and *C6*, but only if this is the tonic of the key.

- **Examples 9-7, 9-8:** *D* Dorian arpeggio

  The Dorian pattern goes with minor chords, in this case with *Dm, Dm7, Dm6, Dm11*, and *Dm13*.

- **Examples 9-9, 9-10:** *F* Lydian and *E* Phrygian arpeggio

  The Phrygian pattern goes over minor chords, in this case *Em* and *Em7*, but only when the tonic of the chord is the 3rd of the key; for instance, *Am7* in the key of *F*. The Lydian pattern goes with major chords, in this case with *F* major, *Fmaj7*, *F6*, and *Fmaj9*.

- **Examples 9-11, 9-12:** *G* Mixolydian arpeggio
- **Examples 9-13, 9-14:** *G* Mixolydian alternative arpeggio

  The Mixolydian pattern goes with dominant 7th chords, in this case with *G7, G9, G11*, and *G13*.

- **Examples 9-15, 9-16:** *A* Aeolian arpeggio

  The Aeolian pattern goes with minor chords when the tonic of the chord is the relative minor of the key, or the 6th. In this case, in the key of *C* major, it would go with *Am, Am7*, and *Am9*.

C Ionian and *B* Locrian Arpeggio Pattern/Position

In order to simplify the infinite possibilities of arpeggios, I've presented them in the same pattern/position format that I used with the modes. Each pattern/position contains two sets of arpeggios, one indicated by circled notes and the other by squares. The shaded notes indicate the root note of each mode. In Examples 9-1 and 9-2, the Ionian arpeggio is indicated by circles and the Locrian arpeggio by squares. These individual arpeggios should be practiced separately.

TRACK 115

Ex. 9-1

TRACK 116

Ex. 9-2

TRACK

Ex. 9-3

TRACK

Ex. 9-4

Fig. 9-3 and Fig. 9-4

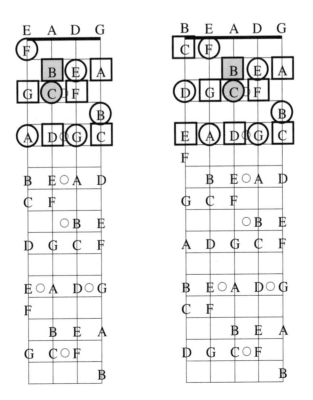

C Ionian Alternative Arpeggio Pattern/Position

TRACK 119

Ex. 9-5

4-string bass

TRACK 120

Ex. 9-6

5-string bass

Fig. 9-5 and Fig. 9-6

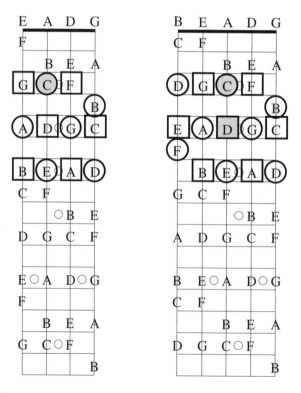

D Dorian Arpeggio Pattern/Position

Ex. 9-7

Ex. 9-8

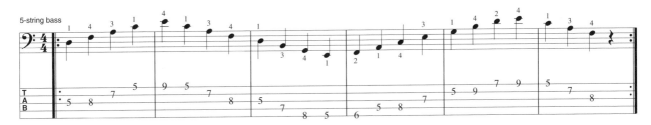

Fig. 9-7 and Fig. 9-8

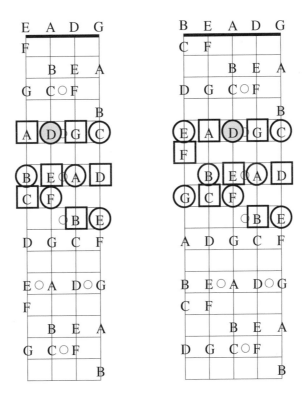

F Lydian and *E* Phrygian Arpeggio Pattern/Position

TRACK **123**

Ex. 9-9

4-string bass

TRACK **124**

Ex. 9-10

5-string bass

Fig. 9-9 and Fig. 9-10

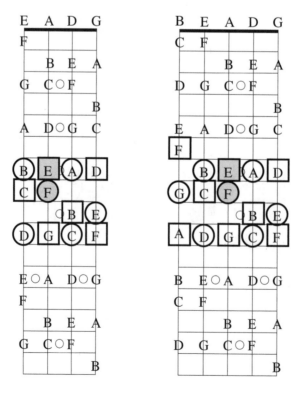

G Mixolydian Arpeggio Pattern/Position

TRACK 125

Ex. 9-11

TRACK 126

Ex. 9-12

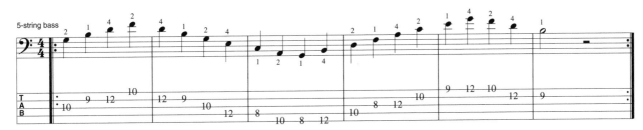

Fig. 9-11 and Fig. 9-12

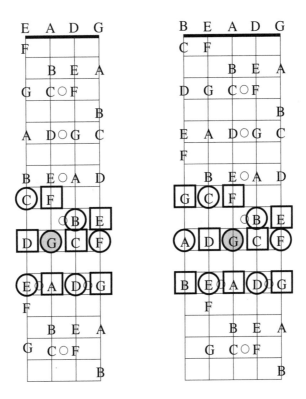

G Mixolydian Alternative Arpeggio Pattern/Position

TRACK 127

Ex. 9-13

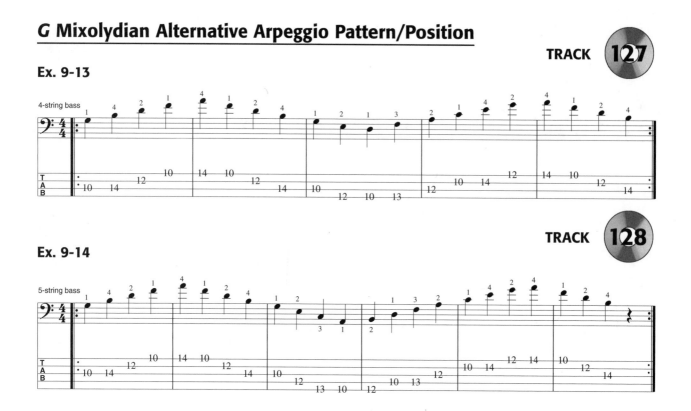

TRACK 128

Ex. 9-14

Fig. 9-13 and Fig. 9-14

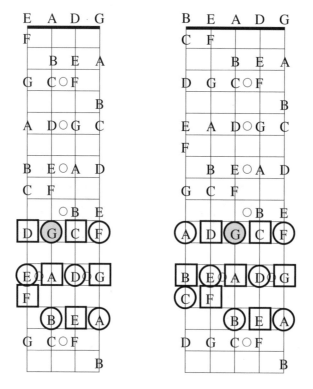

A Aeolian Arpeggio Pattern/Position

TRACK **129**

Ex. 9-15

TRACK **130**

Ex. 9-16

Fig. 9-15 and Fig. 9-16

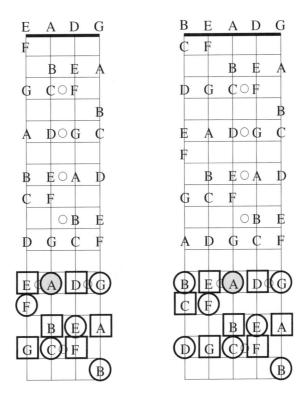

C Harmonic Minor Modes: Arpeggio Patterns/Positions

The Patterns/Positions

- **Examples 10-1, 10-2:** *C* Ionian and *B* Locrian harmonic minor arpeggio
- **Examples 10-3, 10-4:** *C* Ionian harmonic minor arpeggio
- **Examples 10-5, 10-6:** *D* Dorian harmonic minor arpeggio
- **Examples 10-7, 10-8:** *D* Dorian harmonic minor alternative arpeggio
- **Examples 10-9, 10-10:** *E* Spanish Phrygian and *F* Lydian harmonic minor arpeggio

   The Spanish Phrygian is used for dominant-7th chords when the tonic of that chord is the 3rd of the key. In this case, in the key of *C* major, it would go with *E7*, *E7♭9*, *E7♭13*, and *E7♯5*.
- **Examples 10-11, 10-12:** *G♯* Mixolydian harmonic minor arpeggio
- **Examples 10-13, 10-14:** *G♯* Mixolydian harmonic minor alternative arpeggio

   The Mixolydian harmonic minor is a good substitute for the diminished chord. In this case it would go with *G♯dim* or *G♯dim7*.
- **Examples 10-15, 10-16:** *A* Aeolian harmonic minor arpeggio

   The Aeolian harmonic minor is used for minor/major 7th chords when the tonic of the chord is the relative minor, or 6th, of the key. In this case, in the key of *C* major, it would go with *Am/maj7* or *Am/maj9*.

C Ionian and *B* Locrian Harmonic Minor
Arpeggio Pattern/Position

TRACK 131

Ex. 10-1

TRACK 132

Ex. 10-2

Fig. 10-1 and Fig. 10-2

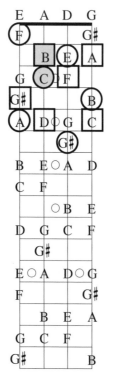
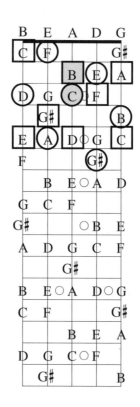

C Ionian Harmonic Minor
Arpeggio Pattern/Position

TRACK 133

Ex. 10-3

TRACK 134

Ex. 10-4

Fig. 10-3 and Fig. 10-4

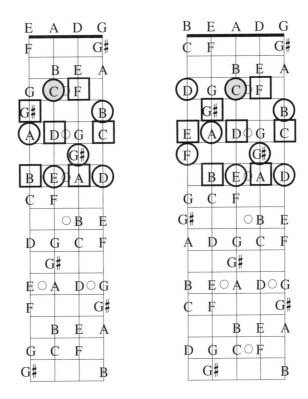

D Dorian Harmonic Minor
Arpeggio Pattern/Position

TRACK 135

Ex. 10-5

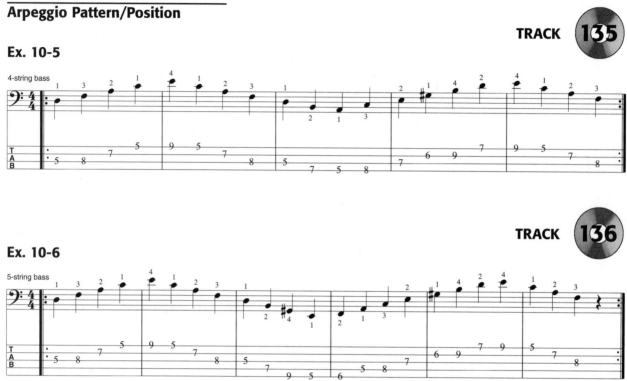

TRACK 136

Ex. 10-6

Fig. 10-5 and Fig. 10-6

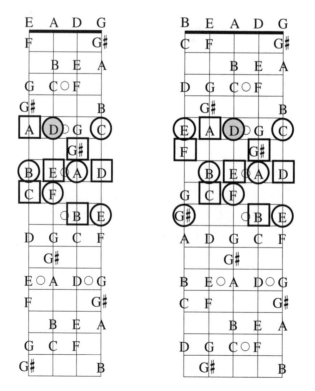

D Dorian Harmonic Minor
Alternative Arpeggio Pattern/Position

Note that the beginning of the arpeggio is identical to the diminished arpeggio. This can be useful for substitutions.

TRACK 137

Ex. 10-7

TRACK 138

Ex. 10-8

Fig. 10-7 and Fig. 10-8

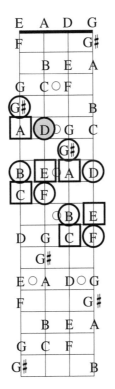

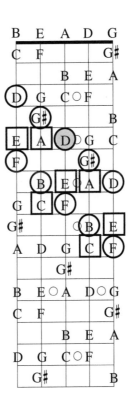

E Spanish Phrygian and *F* Lydian Harmonic Minor
Arpeggio Pattern/Position

TRACK 139

Ex. 10-9

TRACK 140

Ex. 10-10

Fig. 10-9 and Fig. 10-10

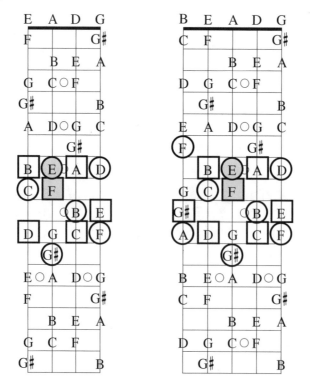

G# Mixolydian Harmonic Minor
Arpeggio Pattern/Position

TRACK 141

Ex. 10-11

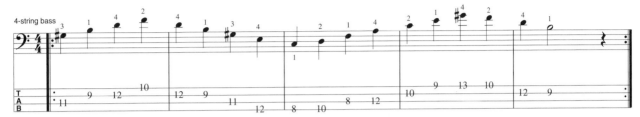

Ex. 10-12

TRACK 142

Fig. 10-11 and Fig. 10-12

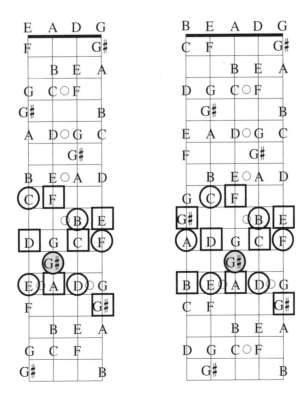

G# Mixolydian Harmonic Minor
Alternative Arpeggio Pattern/Position

TRACK 143

Ex. 10-13

Ex. 10-14

TRACK 144

Fig. 10-13 and Fig. 10-14

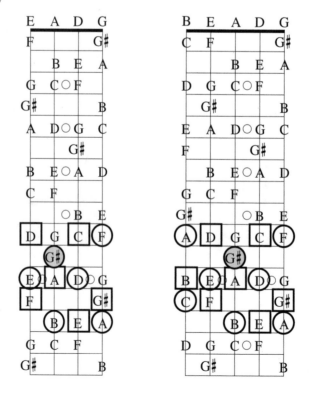

A Aeolian Harmonic Minor
Arpeggio Pattern/Position

TRACK 145

Ex. 10-15

TRACK 146

Ex. 10-16

Fig. 10-15 and Fig. 10-16

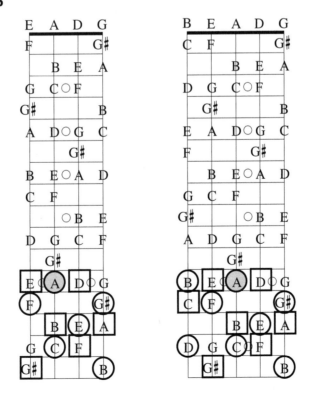

C Melodic Minor Modes:
Arpeggio Patterns/Positions

The Patterns/Positions

- **Examples 11-1, 11-2:** *C* Ionian and *B* Locrian melodic minor arpeggio
- **Examples 11-3, 11-4:** *C* Ionian and *B* Locrian alternative arpeggio

  The Ionian melodic minor goes with minor/major 7th chords. In this case it would go with *Cm/maj7* and *Cm/maj9*.

- **Examples 11-5, 11-6:** *D* Dorian and *E♭* Phrygian melodic minor arpeggio

  The Dorian melodic minor goes with minor 7♭9 chords, in this case with *Dm7♭9*. The Phrygian melodic minor goes with major 7♯5 chords, in this case with *E♭maj7♯5* or *E♭maj9♯5*.

- **Examples 11-7, 11-8:** *F* Lydian and *E♭* Phrygian melodic minor arpeggio

  The Lydian/Mixolydian (see page 45) goes with dominant 7♯11 or ♭5 chords, in this case with *F7♭5* or *F7♯11*.

- **Examples 11-9, 11-10:** *G* Super Mixolydian melodic minor arpeggio
- **Examples 11-11, 11-12:** *G* Super Mixolydian alternative arpeggio

  I like to call the Super Mixolydian the *♭13 scale*. It goes with ♭13 chords, in this case with *G7♭13*.

- **Examples 11-13, 11-14:** *A* Aeolian melodic minor arpeggio

  The Aeolian melodic minor goes with minor 7♭5 chords with a 9, in this case with *Am7♭5/9*.

C Ionian and *B* Locrian Melodic Minor
Arpeggio Pattern/Position

TRACK 147

Ex. 11-1

4-string bass

TRACK 148

Ex. 11-2

5-string bass

Fig. 11-1 and Fig. 11-2

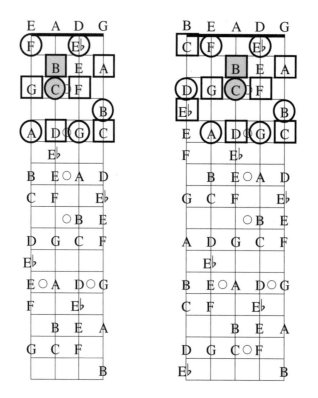

C Ionian and B Locrian
Alternative Arpeggio Pattern/Position

Ex. 11-3

4-string bass

Ex. 11-4

5-string bass

Fig. 11-3 and Fig. 11-4

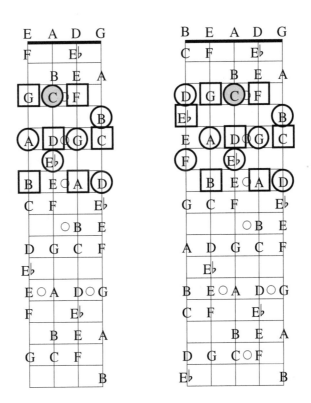

D Dorian and *E*♭ Phrygian Melodic Minor
Arpeggio Pattern/Position

TRACK 151

Ex. 11-5

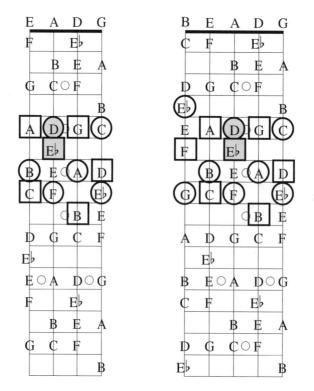

TRACK 152

Ex. 11-6

Fig. 11-5 and Fig. 11-6

F Lydian and *E♭* Phrygian Melodic Minor
Arpeggio Pattern/Position

TRACK 153

Ex. 11-7

TRACK 154

Ex. 11-8

Fig. 11-7 and Fig. 11-8

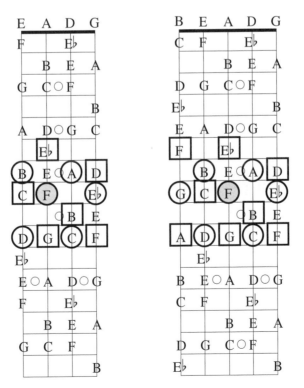

G Super Mixolydian Melodic Minor
Arpeggio Pattern/Position

TRACK 155

Ex. 11-9

TRACK 156

Ex. 11-10

Fig. 11-9 and Fig. 11-10

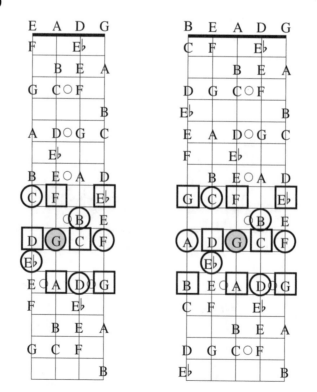

G Super Mixolydian
Alternative Arpeggio Pattern/Position

TRACK 157

Ex. 11-11

TRACK 158

Ex. 11-12

Fig. 11-11 and Fig. 11-12

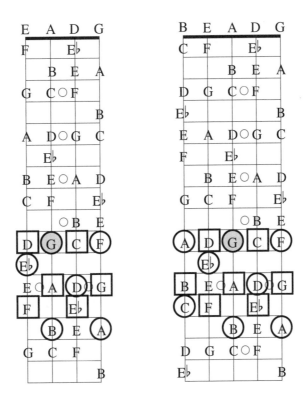

A Aeolian Melodic Minor
Arpeggio Pattern/Position

TRACK 159

Ex. 11-13

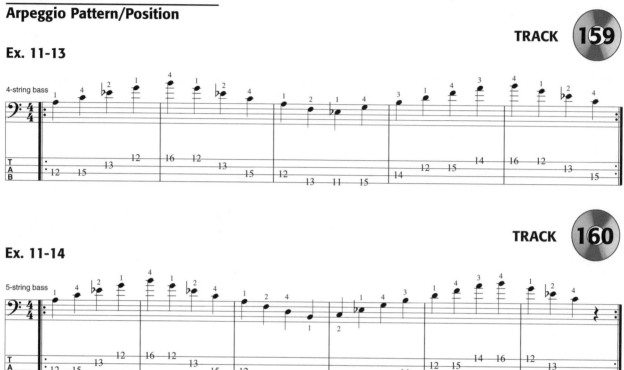

TRACK 160

Ex. 11-14

Fig. 11-13 and Fig. 11-14

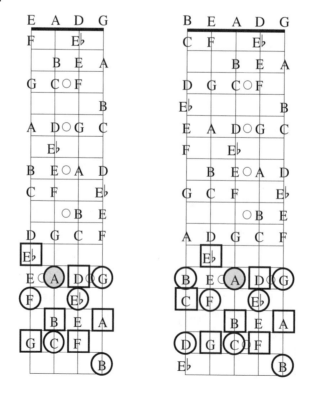

C Harmonic Major Modes:
Arpeggio Patterns/Positions

The Patterns/Positions

- **Examples 12-1, 12-2:** *C* Ionian and *B* Locrian harmonic major arpeggio
- **Examples 12-3, 12-4:** *C* Ionian harmonic major alternative arpeggio
- **Examples 12-5, 12-6:** *D* Dorian harmonic major arpeggio
- **Examples 12-7, 12-8:** *F* Lydian and *E* Phrygian harmonic major arpeggio

  The Phrygian harmonic major mode goes with 7th chords when the tonic of that chord is the 3rd of the key. In this case, in the key of *C* major, it would go with *E7, E7♭9, E7♯9, E7♭13,* and *E7♯5♯9*. The Lydian harmonic major goes with major 7♯11 chords—it's a Lydian scale with a minor 3rd. In this case it would go with *Fm/maj7♯11*. Note that this chord can be mistaken for the diminished/major 7 chord.

- **Examples 12-9, 12-10:** *F* Lydian harmonic major alternative arpeggio
- **Examples 12-11, 12-12:** *G* Mixolydian harmonic major arpeggio
- **Examples 12-13, 12-14:** *G* Mixolydian harmonic major alternative arpeggio

  The Mixolydian harmonic minor goes with 7♭9 chords, in this case with *G7♭9*.

- **Examples 12-15, 12-16:** *A♭* Aeolian harmonic major arpeggio

C Ionian and *B* Locrian Harmonic Major
Arpeggio Pattern/Position

TRACK 161

Ex. 12-1

TRACK 162

Ex. 12-2

Fig. 12-1 and Fig. 12-2

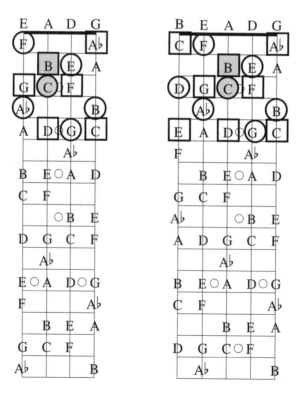

C Ionian Harmonic Major
Alternative Arpeggio Pattern/Position

TRACK 163

Ex. 12-3

TRACK 164

Ex. 12-4

Fig. 12-3 and Fig. 12-4

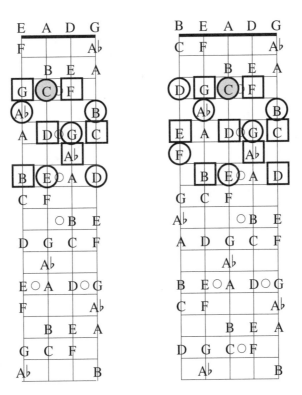

D Dorian Harmonic Major
Arpeggio Pattern/Position

TRACK 165

Ex. 12-5

TRACK 166

Ex. 12-6

Fig. 12-5 and Fig. 12-6

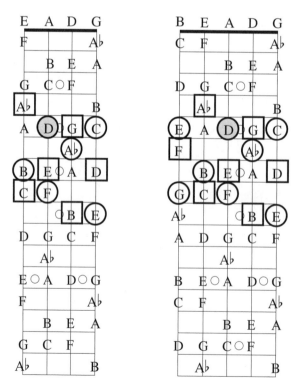

F Lydian and *E* Phrygian Harmonic Major
Arpeggio Pattern/Position

Ex. 12-7

Ex. 12-8

Fig. 12-7 and Fig. 12-8

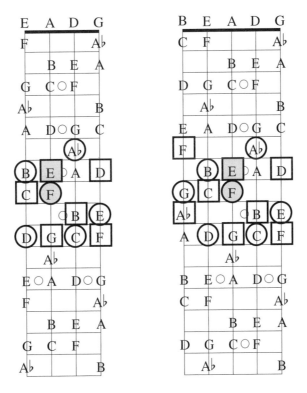

F Lydian Harmonic Major
Alternative Arpeggio Pattern/Position

Note that the beginning of the arpeggio is identical to the diminished arpeggio.
This can be useful for substitutions.

TRACK 169

Ex. 12-9

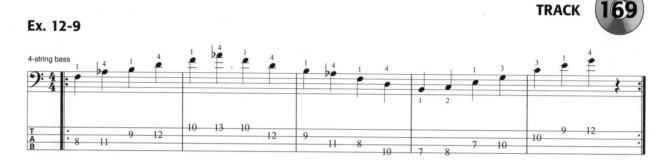

TRACK 170

Ex. 12-10

Fig. 12-9 and Fig. 12-10

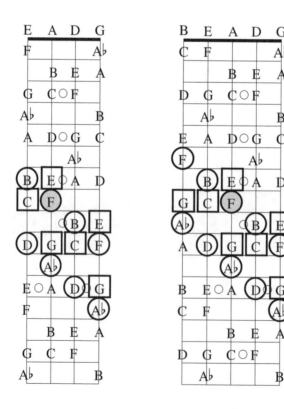

G Mixolydian Harmonic Major
Arpeggio Pattern/Position

Ex. 12-11

Ex. 12-12

Fig. 12-11 and Fig. 12-12

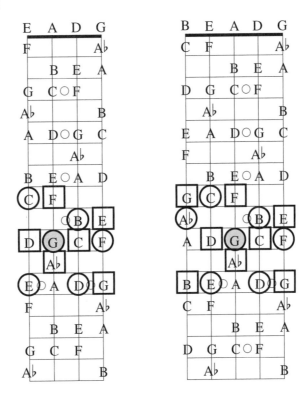

G Mixolydian Harmonic Major
Alternative Arpeggio Pattern/Position

TRACK 173

Ex. 12-13

Ex. 12-14

TRACK 174

Fig. 12-13 and Fig. 12-14

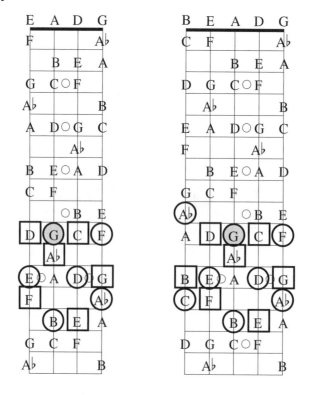

A♭ Aeolian Harmonic Major
Arpeggio Pattern/Position

TRACK

Ex. 12-15

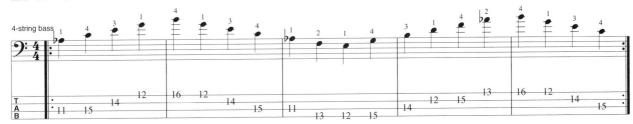

TRACK 176

Ex. 12-16

Fig. 12-15 and Fig. 12-16

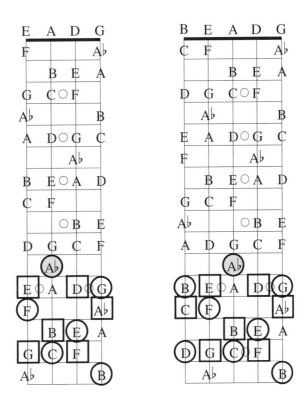

Additional Modes: Arpeggio Patterns/Positions

The Patterns/Positions

- **Examples 13-1, 13-2:** *C* diminished arpeggio

  The diminished scale goes with diminished chords. In this case it would go with *Cdim*, *Cdim7*, and *Cdim/maj7*.

- **Examples 13-3, 13-4:** *C* auxiliary diminished arpeggio

  The auxiliary diminished scale goes with 7♭9 or 7♯9 chords, in this with *C7♭9*, *C7♯9*, *C13♭9*, and *C13♯9*.

- **Examples 13-5, 13-6:** *C* whole-tone arpeggio

  The whole-tone scale goes with augmented and ♯5 chords, in this case with *Caug* and *C7♯5*.

C Diminished
Arpeggio Pattern/Position

TRACK 177

Ex. 13-1

TRACK 178

Ex. 13-2

Fig. 13-1 and Fig. 13-2

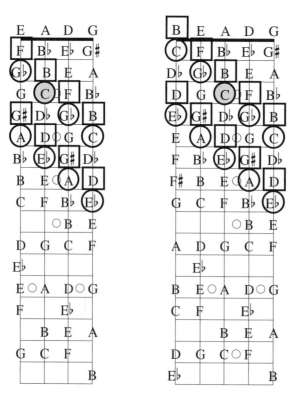

C Auxiliary Diminished
Arpeggio Pattern/Position

TRACK  179

Ex. 13-3

TRACK 180

Ex. 13-4

Fig. 13-3 and Fig. 13-4

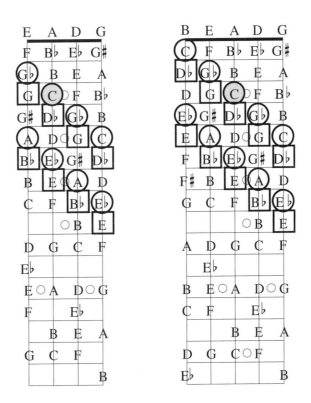

C Whole-Tone
Arpeggio Pattern/Position

TRACK

Ex. 13-5

TRACK

Ex. 13-6

Fig. 13-5 and Fig. 13-6

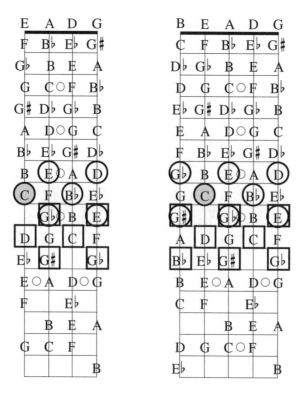

Xtreme! Exercise Examples for Arpeggios

To help you develop good phrasing and melodies, I'll demonstrate a few examples and possibilities with the arpeggios in the key of *C* major. Please apply these to all of the different modes. To get used to the movement, we'll first practice four patterns across the fretboard that are all in the same easy position on the 7th fret.

The Patterns/Positions

- **Ex. 14-1:** Starting on *C*, up and down
- **Ex. 14-2:** Starting on *B*, up and down
- **Ex. 14-3:** Starting from *C*, up and down to *B*
- **Ex. 14-4:** Starting from *B*, up and down to *C*
- **Ex. 14-5:** Playing through all the modes
- **Ex. 14-6:** Playing through all the modes using the extended positions

Starting on *C*, Up and Down

TRACK 183

Ex. 14-1

Starting on *B*, Up and Down

TRACK 184

Ex. 14-2

Starting from *C*, Up and Down to *B*

Ex. 14-3

TRACK 185

Starting from *B*, Up and Down to *C*

Ex. 14-4

TRACK 186

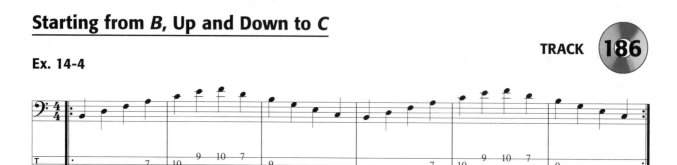

Playing Through All the Modes

This is a great arpeggio pattern that moves up and down the neck.

TRACK 187

Ex. 14-5

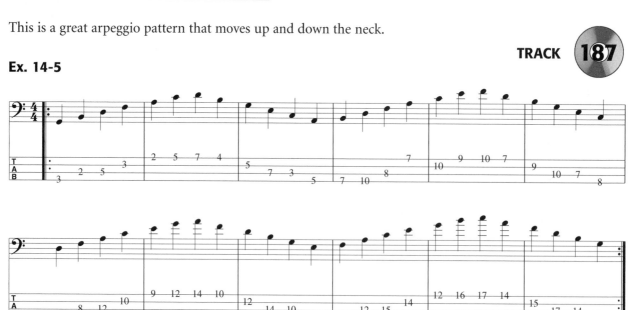

Playing Through All the Modes Using the Extended Positions

This one uses the extended positions to go up the neck.

TRACK 188

Ex. 14-6

Where to Use the Modes

You've learned scale and arpeggio patterns in all of the modes, but where do you use them? Here's the key to matching modes with chords.

Major Modes

These chords	Go with these modes
C, Cadd9, Cadd2, C6, C6/9, Cmaj7, Cmaj9	C Lydian
But when the key is C major	C Ionian
C7, C9, Csus4, C7sus4	C Mixolydian
C11, C11/9, C7/6, C13, C13/9	C Mixolydian
Cmaj7♭5, Cmaj7♭5/9, Cmaj7♯11, Cmaj7♯11/9	C Lydian
C7♭5, C7♭5/9, C7♯11, C7♯11/9	C Lydian-Mixolydian
C7♯5 (or Caug or C+), C whole-tone, C7♭13, C7♭13/9	C Super Mixolydian
C7♭9, C7♯9, C13♭9, C13♯9	C auxiliary diminished
C7♭9, C7♯9, C7♭9♭13, C7♯9♭13, when the root of the chord is the 3rd of the key (A♭ major)	C Spanish Phrygian (harmonic minor) or C Phrygian (harmonic major)
C7♭5/♭9, C7♭5/♯9, C7♯5/♯9, C7♯5/♭9 (or altered)	C Super Locrian (C altered)
C7♯5/♭9, C7♭13♭9, when the root of the chord is the 3rd of the key (A♭ major)	C Spanish Phrygian (harmonic minor)
Cmaj7♯5, Cmaj7♯5/9	C Phrygian melodic minor

Minor Modes

These chords	Go with these modes
Cm, Cm7, Cm9, Cm11	C Dorian
Cm11/9, Cm13, Cm13/9	C Dorian
Cm, Cm7, Cm9, Cm11, Cm11/9, if the root of the chord is the relative minor (in this case C in the key of E♭)	C Aeolian
Cm/maj7, Cm/maj9	C Ionian, or C melodic minor or C Aeolian harmonic minor if the root is the relative minor (in this case C in the key of E♭)
Cm/maj7♯11, Cm/maj9♯11	C Lydian harmonic major
Cdim, Cdim7, Cdim/maj7	C diminished
	C Mixolydian harmonic minor, or C Lydian harmonic major
Cm7♭5 (C half-diminished)	C Locrian
Cm7♭5/9	C Aeolian melodic minor
Cm7♯5	C Aeolian or C Phrygian, depending on the key (E♭ major for Aeolian; A♭ major for Phrygian)
Cm7♭9	C Dorian melodic minor

On the CD

The tracks on the included CD are recorded in both MP3 and WAV formats, playable with audio applications such as QuickTime, Windows Media Player, and RealPlayer, or on disc players that read MP3 files.

Lesson 1

Track 1	Ex. 1–1
Track 2	Ex. 1–2
Track 3	Ex. 1–3
Track 4	Ex. 1–4
Track 5	Ex. 1–5
Track 6	Ex. 1–6
Track 7	Ex. 1–7
Track 8	Ex. 1–8
Track 9	Ex. 1–9
Track 10	Ex. 1–10
Track 11	Ex. 1–11
Track 12	Ex. 1–12
Track 13	Ex. 1–13
Track 14	Ex. 1–14
Track 15	Ex. 1–15
Tracks 16–19	Ex. 1–16
Track 20	Ex. 1–17

Lesson 2

Track 21	Ex. 2–1
Track 22	Ex. 2–2
Track 23	Ex. 2–3
Track 24	Ex. 2–4
Track 25	Ex. 2–5
Track 26	Ex. 2–6
Track 27	Ex. 2–7
Track 28	Ex. 2–8
Track 29	Ex. 2–9
Track 30	Ex. 2–10
Track 31	Ex. 2–11
Track 32	Ex. 2–12
Track 33	Ex. 2–13
Track 34	Ex. 2–14

Lesson 3

Track 35	Ex. 3–1
Track 36	Ex. 3–2
Track 37	Ex. 3–3
Track 38	Ex. 3–4
Track 39	Ex. 3–5
Track 40	Ex. 3–6
Track 41	Ex. 3–7
Track 42	Ex. 3–8

Lesson 4

Track 43	Ex. 4–1
Track 44	Ex. 4–2
Track 45	Ex. 4–3
Track 46	Ex. 4–4
Track 47	Ex. 4–5
Track 48	Ex. 4–6
Track 49	Ex. 4–7
Track 50	Ex. 4–8
Track 51	Ex. 4–9
Track 52	Ex. 4–10
Track 53	Ex. 4–11
Track 54	Ex. 4–12
Track 55	Ex. 4–13
Track 56	Ex. 4–14
Track 57	Ex. 4–15
Track 58	Ex. 4–16
Track 59	Ex. 4–17
Track 60	Ex. 4–18

Lesson 5

Track 61	Ex. 5–1
Track 62	Ex. 5–2
Track 63	Ex. 5–3
Track 64	Ex. 5–4
Track 65	Ex. 5–5
Track 66	Ex. 5–6
Track 67	Ex. 5–7
Track 68	Ex. 5–8
Track 69	Ex. 5–9
Track 70	Ex. 5–10
Track 71	Ex. 5–11
Track 72	Ex. 5–12
Track 73	Ex. 5–13
Track 74	Ex. 5–14
Track 75	Ex. 5–15
Track 76	Ex. 5–16
Track 77	Ex. 5–17
Track 78	Ex. 5–18

Lesson 6

Track 79	Ex. 6–1
Track 80	Ex. 6–2
Track 81	Ex. 6–3
Track 82	Ex. 6–4

Track 83	Ex. 6–5	Track 118	Ex. 9–4	Track 155	Ex. 11–9
Track 84	Ex. 6–6	Track 119	Ex. 9–5	Track 156	Ex. 11–10
Track 85	Ex. 6–7	Track 120	Ex. 9–6	Track 157	Ex. 11–11
Track 86	Ex. 6–8	Track 121	Ex. 9–7	Track 158	Ex. 11–12
Track 87	Ex. 6–9	Track 122	Ex. 9–8	Track 159	Ex. 11–13
Track 88	Ex. 6–10	Track 123	Ex. 9–9	Track 160	Ex. 11–14
Track 89	Ex. 6–11	Track 124	Ex. 9–10		

Lesson 7

Track 90	Ex. 6–12	Track 125	Ex. 9–11	**Lesson 12**	
Track 91	Ex. 6–13	Track 126	Ex. 9–12	Track 161	Ex. 12–1
Track 92	Ex. 6–14	Track 127	Ex. 9–13	Track 162	Ex. 12–2
		Track 128	Ex. 9–14	Track 163	Ex. 12–3
Lesson 7		Track 129	Ex. 9–15	Track 164	Ex. 12–4
Track 93	Ex. 7–1	Track 130	Ex. 9–16	Track 165	Ex. 12–5
Track 94	Ex. 7–2			Track 166	Ex. 12–6
Track 95	Ex. 7–3	**Lesson 10**		Track 167	Ex. 12–7
Track 96	Ex. 7–4	Track 131	Ex. 10–1	Track 168	Ex. 12–8
Track 97	Ex. 7–5	Track 132	Ex. 10–2	Track 169	Ex. 12–9
Track 98	Ex. 7–6	Track 133	Ex. 10–3	Track 170	Ex. 12–10
		Track 134	Ex. 10–4	Track 171	Ex. 12–11
Lesson 8		Track 135	Ex. 10–5	Track 172	Ex. 12–12
Track 99	Ex. 8–1	Track 136	Ex. 10–6	Track 173	Ex. 12–13
Track 100	Ex. 8–2	Track 137	Ex. 10–7	Track 174	Ex. 12–14
Track 101	Ex. 8–3	Track 138	Ex. 10–8	Track 175	Ex. 12–15
Track 102	Ex. 8–4	Track 139	Ex. 10–9	Track 176	Ex. 12–16
Track 103	Ex. 8–5	Track 140	Ex. 10–10		
Track 104	Ex. 8–6	Track 141	Ex. 10–11	**Lesson 13**	
Track 105	Ex. 8–7	Track 142	Ex. 10–12	Track 177	Ex. 13–1
Track 106	Ex. 8–8	Track 143	Ex. 10–13	Track 178	Ex. 13–2
Track 107	Ex. 8–9	Track 144	Ex. 10–14	Track 179	Ex. 13–3
Track 108	Ex. 8–10	Track 145	Ex. 10–15	Track 180	Ex. 13–4
Track 109	Ex. 8–11	Track 146	Ex. 10–16	Track 181	Ex. 13–5
Track 110	Ex. 8–12			Track 182	Ex. 13–6
Track 111	Ex. 8–13	**Lesson 11**			
Track 112	Ex. 8–14	Track 147	Ex. 11–1	**Lesson 14**	
Track 113	Ex. 8–15	Track 148	Ex. 11–2	Track 183	Ex. 14–1
Track 114	Ex. 8–16	Track 149	Ex. 11–3	Track 184	Ex. 14–2
		Track 150	Ex. 11–4	Track 185	Ex. 14–3
Lesson 9		Track 151	Ex. 11–5	Track 186	Ex. 14–4
Track 115	Ex. 9–1	Track 152	Ex. 11–6	Track 187	Ex. 14–5
Track 116	Ex. 9–2	Track 153	Ex. 11–7	Track 188	Ex. 14–6
Track 117	Ex. 9–3	Track 154	Ex. 11–8		

Acknowledgments

Special thanks to Emmy, Richard Johnston, Mackie, MOTU, ART, DigiTech, Monster Cable, and Tannoy.

Bunny Brunel plays exclusively on Carvin Bunny Brunel model basses and amps, with La Bella strings.

For more information on other Bunny Brunel products go to www.bunnybrunel.com.

About the Author

Discovered by Chick Corea, Bernard "Bunny" Brunel was one of the original "gunslingers of the bass" along with Stanley Clarke, Jaco Pastorius, and Jeff Berlin. Brunel has recorded and performed with a who's who of musical giants including Herbie Hancock, Wayne Shorter, Tony Williams, Al Jarreau, Natalie Cole, Larry Coryell, Al Di Meola, Mike Stern, and Joe Farrell.

Besides his work as a performer, Brunel is also a composer, arranger, and designer. As a soundtrack composer he collaborated with Clint Eastwood in creating "Claudia's Theme," the main theme for the award-winning film *Unforgiven*. He has also worked on several television shows, including the popular *Highlander* series. As a designer, Bunny created a line of electric bass guitars for Carvin, and he has designed an electric upright bass.

Bunny's solo albums include *Momentum, Ivanhoe, Touch, Dedication, For You to Play, L.A. Zoo,* and *Café au Lait*. His albums with Tony MacAlpine, Brian Auger, and Dennis Chambers in the fusion group CAB include the Grammy-nominated *CAB2* and the recent *CAB4*.

Bunny regularly gives seminars on his unique approach to electric bass, and he has created several videos and instructional books, including *Bunny Brunel's Power Bass: Soloing Secrets* [Backbeat]. For information log on to www.bunnybrunel.com.

WHEN IT COMES TO THE BASS, WE WROTE THE BOOK.

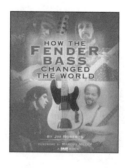